Girl, Shake it Off

Unlocking the Power of Self-Love, Courage, and Connection : Your Guide To .A Fuller Life.

Inspired By

Taylor Swift

Wendy Raymond

This book is published by Therapy Seminary Publishers.

Paperback Edition: **ISBN: 978-1-963674-29-3**

First Edition: 2024

Table of Contents

A Word From The Author

Hello! I'm Becky. Once, I was a housewife sacrificing my dreams, trapped in a failing marriage. Today, I'm a certified therapist and author, fueling women worldwide with the strength I forged from my own struggles. Think your life's a dumpster fire? Hold my coffee. I've been there, battled through the flames, and I'm here to show you how to do the same. Rejections, mistakes, grief, indecision, bad decisions – they tried to bury me, but they didn't know I was a seed. Ready to ditch the baggage, find your inner badass, and make life your masterpiece? Buckle up, buttercup, this rollercoaster's about to get wild!

INTRODUCTION: Hey There, Beautiful Journey Ahead

When the idea of this book started to take root in my mind, I envisioned it as an anthem, much like the empowering beats of Taylor Swift's "Shake It Off." That song, with its infectious energy and unapologetic embrace of self, became more than just a backdrop to my life; it was a call to action.

Picture a bright, unstoppable day in the summer of 2021, after the Covid 19 Pandemic. I remember it was a Thursday because that's when our team gathers for our weekly brainstorm, a ritual that finds us at our most creative and unabashedly silly. The sun was pouring in, making our meeting room glow with possibilities. We always kick things off with a dance, believing firmly that the right song can shake off any residue of doubt or hesitation. That week, it was my turn to play DJ, a role I relish for the chance to set the tone.

The first chords of "Shake It Off" filled the room, and it was like a switch flipped. There's something about Taylor Swift's defiance, her cheeky acknowledgment of the critics and naysayers, paired with the commitment to dance through it all, that feels like a personal manifesto. At that moment, my team and I were not just preparing for another meeting; we were declaring our resilience, our joy, and our freedom from the judgment of others.

This song, with its catchy beat and bold lyrics, became my anthem, my reminder that the opinions of others are just background noise. It followed me everywhere—blasting through speakers as I worked out, humming in my earbuds as I navigated the challenges of daily life, even toned down in a lullaby version I'd hum to my kids at night. My dedication to keeping it on repeat was a testament to its impact. It's rare to find a song that so perfectly encapsulates the journey of shedding the weight of others' expectations to find your own rhythm.

And so, inspired by Taylor's message, I began to wonder: What was I holding onto that I needed to shake off? What fears, doubts, and old narratives were keeping me from dancing to my own beat?

The truth is, like so many of us, I've been tangled in a web of trying to please everyone, of muting my own desires to fit into a neatly prescribed box. But no more. This book is my journey, and hopefully yours, of breaking free from those chains. It's about recognizing that the only approval you need is your own, that the dreams you've tucked away for a "someday" that never comes deserve the spotlight now.

In these pages, I invite you to join me in a dance of liberation. Let's explore what it means to live boldly, to set audacious goals, and to embrace the beauty of who we are without apology. From the trenches of self-doubt to the peaks of personal triumph, this is our anthem. Let's shake off the shackles of expectation and step into the light of self-acceptance and ambition.

As we move through this journey together, remember that it's not about perfection. It's about progress. It's about the courage to be yourself in a world that's constantly trying to make you something else. It's about shaking off the "shoulds" and "what ifs" to uncover the vibrant, limitless person you were always meant to be.

So hey, girl, let's shake it off together. Let's dance into a future where we're not just surviving but thriving, on our own terms. Welcome to the beginning of your most exhilarating adventure yet.

Chapter One:

Embracing Today: Your Happiness Journey
Discover joy in the present and the small steps that lead to big changes.

"It's not the load that breaks you down, it's the way you carry it." — Lena Horne

One time I was at a grocery store, cruising the aisles like a NASCAR driver after my third kid just hurled her blueberry muffin down my shirt. My other child was screaming in the cart, and my toddler hanging off my leg wailing for a juice box, and to top it off, my oldest just face-planted in the produce while trying to lick a watermelon.

It was a freaking circus. My heart was pounding, my shirt had mysterious stains, and the sweet cashier smiling at me might as well be on Mars. I felt it rising— that wave of hot, prickly shame. *Why can't I get my act together? Does anyone else's life look like a dumpster fire?*

Girl, that was me some years ago. Plenty of times. And the thing is, life is messy. Kids are messy. Motherhood? It's the ultimate hot mess express, most days. But here's what I came to learn, after many spectacular mom-fails: it's not about having it all together, it's how we CHOOSE to handle the chaos.

You see, life hands us a ton of stuff we didn't ask for. Work stress, tantrums, unexpected bills, you name it. We could let each burden weigh us down until we're hunched over and miserable. OR, we could adjust the straps. It's like switching from a tattered old knapsack to a sleek, supportive backpack. Distributes the weight better, doesn't it?

That's what I had to figure out. How to wear my burdens a little lighter. It took a while, a LOT of coffee-fueled chats with friends who were in the trenches with me, and maybe a good cry or two. But you know what? I found my version of that supportive backpack:

- **Perspective**. I realized most moms feel chaotic, just some are better at hiding it. It's okay to have days when your hair resembles a squirrel's nest... we've earned it!

- **Humor**. Laughter is my superpower. Finding the ridiculousness in a toddler meltdown can shift the whole vibe.

- **Asking for help**. Delegating isn't weak, it's smart. Asking a friend to grocery shop together was a game-changer.

Workbook

1. **Name Your Burdens:** Jot down EVERY stressor, from big (finances) to weirdly specific (that Lego piece you ALWAYS step on). Seeing them on paper is the first step.

2. **"Backpack" Check:** Are you dragging around burdens that aren't yours to carry? Guilt over not being a Pinterest-perfect mom? Comparing yourself to the Insta-influencer down the street? Ditch that baggage!

3. **Find Your Support System:** Which friend makes you laugh the hardest? Who's always got your back? Reach out – sharing the weight is key.

Remember girl, Motherhood isn't a perfectly curated photo album. It's a wild, beautiful ride – bumps, spills, blueberry stains, and all. Choose to carry it with a little less burden, and a little more laughter, and you'll find a whole new level of joy in the journey.

Chapter Two

Begin Now: The Magic Of Starting

Overcome procrastination by embracing the beauty of beginning, no matter where you are

"You are confined only by the walls you build yourself." – Andrew Murphy

We've all been there. Counting diets like notches on a belt, making grand plans only to crumble when it's time to walk the walk. Remember that "New Year, New Me" energy that fizzles out before Valentine's Day? Yeah, I feel that deep in my soul.

You talk about running that marathon, writing that book, whatever your heart desires... but those desires stay just that, desires. Because, honey, talking about doing something and actually doing it are two planets apart.

We're great at justifying why we flake. The kids, work, that surprise project that pops up... excuses are always waiting, arms wide open. But what about the promises we made to ourselves? They get buried under the daily grind, and honestly, that's gotta stop.

Society gives us a free pass for not trying enough. Magazines hype us up, then focus on the recovery when we fall, not the strength to stay up. But where were those same magazines when we were learning to walk? Did someone write a "Ten Tips on Getting Back Up When You Can't Even Crawl" article when we were babies? Nope. We got cheers and praise while we figured it out. Somewhere along the way, we forgot how to give ourselves that same grace and grit.

But let's flip that script for a moment. Remember your girlfriend's night? When you jump on the treadmill after a long day? Girl, that's a taste of the power you hold. It's those little victories that become a habit, a new way of being. Imagine the Becky who doesn't cancel on herself. That's where the true magic of starting lies.

Workbook

1. The Past Doesn't Define You: Take out a pen and paper (yes, old-school!), and jot down 5 times you started something but didn't finish. Next, list ONE reason why you gave up – be brutally honest. See any patterns? That's where we can start the change.

2. Accountability Time: Think of that ONE friend who always keeps their word. You know the type - punctual, reliable if they say they'll do something, consider it done. Find your version of this person and spill your guts. Tell them one goal you want to achieve, and ask them to help you stay on track.

3. Baby Steps Are Still Steps: We often fail because we dream too big, too fast. That marathon? Amazing goal, but let's start smaller. How about committing to a 15-minute walk, three days a week? Schedule it in your calendar like a non-negotiable meeting. Once in three days feel routine, bump it up. It's the consistency, not the intensity, that will build your "I keep my word" muscle.

It is a positive thing that you have the desire to change. That's already a step ahead! But now's the time to trade the talking for the doing. It won't be perfect, but that's okay. Imagine how incredible it will feel to be that YOU who starts something and sees it through. You got this!

Chapter Three

You Are Enough: Building Self-Love
Learn to see your inherent worth and embrace your imperfections as strengths

"The truth is rarely pure, and never simple." - Oscar Wilde

The air crackled around me, not the kind of charged atmosphere you get before a storm, but the unnerving sort before the bomb drops. It's been hanging over me for weeks now – my husband, Matt, avoiding eye contact, staying late at work, strange phone calls ending the minute I walk through the door. All the classic signs, the awful clichés of a spouse ready to drop the "I'm leaving you" hammer.

I am not a stupid woman. Far from it. Most people would call me sharp, quick-witted, and maybe even a little intimidating. I built myself a career from the ground up, one relentless step after another. People rely on me. At work, I'm the one juggling ten flaming chainsaws while everyone else stands in awe. And at home? Well, I may not be baking cookies, but I *am* the one paying the mortgage and making sure the kids' college funds are on track.

But right now, in this stupid, brightly lit kitchen with Matt's tense back turned towards me, I feel twelve years old again, a scrawny kid with her heart beating like a trapped bird. Maybe it's that same girl, desperate to be seen and loved, who still lurks somewhere inside me.

The truth is, there's never been a time when I *didn't* feel a little bit on the edge. Maybe it was being the odd one out in our small town, the daughter of the eccentric professor, the girl who preferred books to dances. Or maybe it's always been hardwired into me. What I do know is that the harder I fight to fit in, to belong, somehow the more alone I feel.

Matt was the safe harbor. Kind, dependable, a little dull even. He'd been my rock for fifteen years. We weren't a whirlwind romance, but rather a slow-burning flame, a comfortable warmth. He was proud of my success and never felt threatened the way some men do. He saw me, really saw me, or at least I desperately wanted to believe so. And that's why the fear now is paralyzing. If even Matt turns away... what then?

"Matt?" My voice cracks, a stupid, whimpering sound I hate. I clear my throat and try again. "We need to talk."

He turns, but it's the way he doesn't quite fully look at me that seals it. He's been building his wall, brick by brick, just as I've been mustering the courage to breach it. My pulse quickens, fight-or-flight kicking in. But here's the other thing: I'm not just a scrawny kid anymore, I'm a woman who has weathered storms before. Deep down, there's a sliver of iron – forged through hard-won confidence in other areas, though never tested here, not like this.

"Don't do this, Becky," he says, his voice almost a plea.

And suddenly, I'm done. Done with the fear, the tiptoeing around the ugly truth, the desperate clinging to something that may have been a pretty lie all along. My voice comes out steady, stronger than I expected.

"Do what, Matt? Stay in a half-marriage? Pretend everything's fine out of fear? I don't *do* that, not anymore."

He flinches. I take an involuntary step closer. I'd say I want the truth, but am I even sure anymore? The truth isn't a pristine package. Truths are tangled and twisty, nuanced in ways I'm afraid to explore.

But maybe... maybe it's time. Maybe this bomb that's about to detonate my life isn't about destruction at all; maybe it's the messy chance to build something from the rubble. Something truer, something where I truly know my own worth, whether I end up alone or not.

"Tell me," I say. The words settle between us. Not a plea, not a demand, but a choice, an assertion. My voice doesn't shake. I don't recognize the woman speaking, and it feels thrilling, terrifying, and more alive than I have in years.

The pause stretches, Matt finally meets my eyes, and it's there...all the confirmation I didn't want. There's an apology in his expression, the barest hint of pity too, and I hate that even more than the betrayal.

"Becky, it's...complicated," he starts. That classic, gutless, infuriating word. I hold up a hand, stopping him. "Don't. Let's ditch the clichés, okay? Do you love someone else?" My voice is even now, almost clinical.

A pained sort of silence. Then, finally, a barely audible

"yes." The word hangs between us, sharp as broken

glass. But oddly, instead of the shattering I expected,

there's a flicker, not of relief, but a strange sort of

clarity. "Okay then," I say, and he seems genuinely

surprised that I'm not screaming, throwing dishes,

doing what wronged wives do on TV. "Let's talk

logistics, financials, the kids." He blinks. "Becky, I...

didn't think...." He trails off, looking lost. And that's it:

he thought I'd crumble, plead. That I'd make his

choice easy. Well, hell has officially frozen over. "Matt,

what you did was lousy," I say, my voice rising a little,

the anger fueling me now, making me strong. "But I

am not going to let this break me. I will get through

this. The kids will get through this – and better to see

their parents happy even if it's separate, than to live in

this charade."

He's nodding now, maybe starting to catch up to the

new reality. Later that night, collapsed on my side of

our too-big bed, I finally let the tears come. Not for him, but for the girl inside me – the one who always feared she wasn't enough. Turns out, she was wrong. All along.

Workbook

1. Think about someone you pedestalized: a past love, a friend, a mentor...What qualities did you project onto them? Now, consider those same qualities inside yourself.

2. Often, we get stuck looking outward for validation. Write the pep talk you wish you could hear from a fiercely loving friend. What would they tell you about your strengths and worth?

Action Step: Make a list of three things you want to become better at (not things to fix, but skills to grow). Commit to one small action today to start down that path. It could be as simple as researching a class or signing up for a free online tutorial.

Chapter Four

Together We Rise: Celebrating Each Other
Find strength in community and the power of lifting each other up

"Sometimes the bravest and most important thing you can do is just show up." – Brené Brown

It took three bottles of wine and a playlist alternating between 90s angst anthems and self-empowerment pop for Sarah and Jess to get me out the door. Six months post-divorce and I was still a master at building fortresses of solitude out of takeout boxes and Netflix binges.

"You can live like a heartbroken loner, Becky," Sarah chirped, shoving me towards a mirror, "But trust me, those sweatpants have served their purpose."

I glanced at the reflection. Not terrible, but 'glow' and 'lively' were definitely not on the menu. Yet, my friends wouldn't budge, dragging me to a tiny support group gathering tucked away in a community center.

Walking into that room, heavy with the scent of stale coffee and nervous energy, felt like jumping off a cliff. A circle of chairs loomed, occupied by people who wore their pain far more openly than I ever would. A woman with kind, tired eyes beckoned me over. Her name tag said 'Elaine'.

"First time?" she whispered.

I nodded, throat tight.

"Me too," she admitted with a wry smile. "Scary as hell, right?"

And it was. Scary and awkward and absolutely necessary. As stories flowed around that circle, I saw my own mirrored in a dozen variations: betrayal, fear, crippling self-doubt. Every head nod, every squeezed hand, was an unspoken, "I understand. I've been there."

Elaine, with her failed business and shattered marriage, showed me strength doesn't mean steeliness, but rather the raw courage to keep showing up.

There was Tim, whose quiet grief for his late wife cut deep. He taught me heartbreak comes in many forms, and loss doesn't make you less deserving of new beginnings.

And then, there was me. Not the woman who'd built her identity around a relationship, but someone learning to stand on her own two feet. Each time I forced myself to share a sliver of my mess, the room held space for it. Shame turned to something softer, lighter.

Those Tuesday nights became my lifeline. This ragtag group didn't have answers, but they knew the right questions. We became cheerleaders, therapists, and walking reminders that "survive" wasn't the end goal. 'Thrive' was still possible.

One year later, I led my own workshop: Divorce, Finances, and Finding Your Footing. It's packed, and I'm terrified and exhilarated all at once. I show them spreadsheets but also vulnerability. We talk about practical steps AND permission to not feel okay.

Before I start, Sarah, Jess, and Elaine are there, beaming up at me. They hold my gaze as I begin, "See these faces? This is my community. They lifted me when I couldn't lift myself. You will find yours too..."

Because rising isn't a solo mission. We find strength in numbers, in flawed, brave souls who refuse to let one another fall. Alone, we're breakable, but together, we become a force.

Workbook

1. Picture a person who always offers you support. What qualities do you admire most about them? Do you possess any of those qualities yourself?

2. What's one area, however small, where you'd like to support someone else? Is there a friend struggling, a neighbor who could use a hand?

Action Step: Commit! Reach out to one person you know might need encouragement. An offer to listen, a small act of kindness – these create ripples.

Chapter Five

Self-Love First: Beyond Romantic Love
Understand the importance of loving yourself before seeking fulfillment in others

"How you love yourself is how you teach others to love you." – Rupi Kaur

The online dating profiles blurred together like a bad watercolor painting. "Adventurous foodie seeking a soulmate." "Book nerd with a heart of gold, looking for my Mr. Darcy." My cynical sigh echoed around my silent apartment. Swipe left, swipe left... ugh, swipe left again.

It'd been two years since the divorce, and the well-meaning chorus of "you'll find someone again" was starting to sound like the world's worst earworm. Truth be told, jumping back into the dating pool wasn't about finding 'the one'; it was more about not finding myself alone.

My therapist, bless her patient soul, would point out the problem here. "Becky, you're still defining yourself by your relationship status. Until you change that, even the perfect partner is just a band-aid." Ouch.

The thing is, I'd always been the 'half of a whole' type of person. From high school sweethearts to moving in with Matt right out of college, I seamlessly transitioned from one relationship to the next. A master of compromise, expert in accommodating others' needs. But who was *I* underneath all that?

That question sent me on an unexpected journey, a messy and often frustrating self-excavation. First, it was a brutal purge. I cleared out the boxes of Matt's old stuff, donated half my wardrobe (turns out, floral maxi dresses weren't really 'me'), and finally purged my phone of numbers I'd never call.

Next, came the tentative filling of the blank spaces. I tried everything, with varying degrees of awkwardness – painting classes (more splatter on me than on the canvas), salsa lessons (two left feet confirmed), and joining a book club that mostly debated the merits of celebrity gossip.

Some things fizzled out; others stuck. What surprised me was the joy of rediscovering myself purely on my own terms. Hikes where I'd talk out loud to nobody just because I could. Staying up late to devour a gripping novel. Turns out, Becky, when left to her own devices, was pretty damn interesting company.

Of course, there were setbacks: lonely Friday nights filled with the ghosts of old routines, the sting of seeing another one of Matt's Facebook updates about his happy new life. It wasn't linear, this path to self-love. More like two steps forward, one sideways, sometimes a full-blown stumble back.

But with each tentative step, something shifted. I started saying 'no' to things that drained me – forced family gatherings and the pitying looks from old friends. I learned that boundaries were a form of self-care, not selfishness. There was a kind of power in that.

Then, came Ryan. Cute, funny, with a shared love of obscure documentaries. Our first few dates were... fun. But there was no frantic rush, no pressure to fill a void. I chose when to share the vulnerable parts, and I saw him fully, not as a potential savior.

"You're different," he said one night over shared tapas plates. "Not jaded, exactly, but... there's a strength to you now."

And there it was: proof that the work was paying off. I wasn't healed - scars don't disappear - but I was more solid. Ryan wasn't a puzzle piece to complete me; it was more like we were two separate puzzles, sometimes fitting together, sometimes existing side-by-side. That, it turned out, was a far healthier kind of love.

Workbook

1. Think about how you typically approach relationships. Are you quick to adjust yourself to someone new? What would it feel like to 'hold your shape' a little more?
2. What's one activity, forgotten hobby, or interest you used to enjoy? Is there space to bring a little bit of that back into your life?

Action Step: Make a "Me-First" List. Ten things that bring you genuine joy, regardless of having a partner. This isn't selfish; it's refilling your own cup.

Remember, self-love isn't a destination, it's a lifelong practice. Some days will be easier than others, and that's okay.

Chapter Six

The Power Of 'Yes': Opening New Doors
Learn to embrace opportunities and the transformative power of saying yes to yourself

"And the day came when the risk to remain tight in a bud was more painful than the risk it took to blossom." –
Anaïs Nin

The email sat in my inbox, a little digital grenade threatening to blow up my neatly constructed world. "Conference Speaker Needed: Finance Strategies for Women Entrepreneurs." It should have been a hard pass. Public speaking? Exposing my financial expertise to actual, successful people? My inner critic started a choir of doubt: "You'll stumble over your words... You don't have the experience... They'll laugh you off the stage..."

Yet, there was a niggling curiosity, a tiny flame refusing to be extinguished. Sure, I was good at my job, an ace with budgets and spreadsheets. But something about the idea of sharing that knowledge, maybe even inspiring others, pulled at me.

It was my newly single friend, Jess, who finally pushed me. "Becky, think of all those women you help at work, those who felt so lost about money after a divorce. Imagine scaling that. One 'yes' could change lives."

The thing about change is that it rarely comes dressed in comfortable pajamas. I spent sleepless nights, my living room turned into a makeshift stage with my cat as the unimpressed audience. I bought an actual pantsuit (my first in a decade!) and invested in coaching sessions that slowly chipped away at the fear.

The day of the conference arrived, a whirlwind of sleek professional women and imposter syndrome. Just before my talk, I caught sight of my reflection. Not the Becky in yoga pants and messy bun, but a woman who looked... capable.

I took the stage, and the first few minutes were a blur of adrenaline and remembering to breathe. But then I saw them, the faces in the crowd: hopeful, curious, some mirroring my own anxieties. A shift happened then. I wasn't performing; I was connecting.

I spoke about investment strategies, yes, but also about the courage to take those first steps. I shared the mistakes I'd made, and the fear that still crept in at times. The room started nodding along, some even jotting notes. Afterward, a line of women waited by the podium to talk.

"You made me feel understood," one woman said, her eyes bright. "Like, I'm not alone in this."

Another, a budding business owner, asked for my card and then beamed, "I was terrified of the numbers side. Now, I think I can actually do this!"

It was then that I realized the true power of that one 'yes'. It wasn't about ego, or being some flawless expert. It was about stepping outside my comfort zone, and trusting in potential I hadn't yet fully seen. In doing so, I sparked something in others, and in the flickering light of their excitement, I found a new glimmer in myself too.

The offers started coming. Blog requests, more conference spots, inquiries about creating an online course. Suddenly, that small, safe world I'd built felt a bit too tight. This new path was unknown, exhilarating, and undoubtedly terrifying. But somewhere along the way, fear became a less formidable opponent, and possibility whispered louder than doubt.

Three years later, my business is thriving. I'm still no fan of the stage, but I've learned to channel the nervous energy into something purposeful. The best part is the emails I get, the women who say "Because of you..." and then detail their own triumphs, big and small. It turns out, that self-doubt never fully departs, but 'yes' can drown it out.

Workbook

1. Think of a time you let fear stop you from trying something. What was the cost of that missed opportunity? How would your life look had you said 'yes' instead?

2. What's a 'small Yes' lurking at the edge of your comfort zone? Maybe a new class, learning a skill, or striking up a conversation with a stranger.

Action Step: Make a "Hell Yes" and a "Hell No" List. Things that excite you vs. those that drain you. Prioritize the "Hell Yes".

Chapter Seven

Embracing Intimacy: Your Desires Matter
Navigate the complexities of intimacy with confidence and self-awareness

"The way to change the world is to change the way we experience our bodies, not just the laws that govern them." – Eve Ensler

The sex therapist looked way too young to be dispensing life-changing advice, but her eyes were warm. It took more courage than I'd like to admit to be sitting here, next to Ryan on that overly cheerful couch.

"We're good," Ryan had insisted when I first brought it up. "Our sex life is fine."

But 'fine' was a long way from the passionate connection I yearned for. We'd slipped into predictable patterns, a perfunctory routine rather than something truly soul-stirring. There was love between us, absolutely, but the spark had become more of a gentle flicker. My hesitancy to bring it up stemmed from shame more than anything. Shouldn't good partners just intuitively know what the other wants?

Sarah, ever the champion of direct communication, had other thoughts. "Becky, talking about sex is like talking about your finances. Uncomfortable, but necessary if you want things to improve." With her support (and a few glasses of wine), I'd finally broached the subject with Ryan, who seemed more surprised than upset.

Now here we were, spilling our guts to a stranger. The therapist, Dr. Ellis, normalized it all quickly. "Many couples hit roadblocks with intimacy," she explained. "It's about far more than mechanics; it's about connecting deeply, desires, expectations, vulnerabilities... which we rarely articulate consciously."

We spent sessions diving into what we liked, disliked, and fantasized about but never actually verbalized. It was awkward at first, blushing and stammering over words that shouldn't have felt so loaded. But with gentle guidance, a new language emerged.

Ryan, it turned out, was far more into the slow build of anticipation, of feeling truly desired, than I'd ever realized. I discovered an often-buried hunger for something a bit rougher, a playfulness I'd mistaken for immaturity in my past. These weren't shameful secrets, just facets we'd kept hidden, even from ourselves.

The changes weren't immediate or earth-shattering. More like tentative explorations, an added touch here, a whispered question there. It was in the giggling after fumbled attempts, in reading suggestions out loud from a dog-eared book we'd found, in learning that vulnerability could be its own kind of sexy.

There was the night Ryan blindfolded me, filling the room with the smoky scent of a candle I usually found too 'girly'. When he slipped off the blindfold, he was kneeling before me, a playful gleam in his eyes. It was the most turned-on I'd felt in ages.

Yet, the biggest shift was inside me. I'd always prided myself on being a 'giving' partner, molding myself to what I thought the other person wanted. It was a revelation to acknowledge my own desires, and even more startling to voice them without feeling I owed an apology afterwards.

The truth was, Ryan wasn't shocked by my desires; rather, he seemed ignited by my willingness to share them. It turned out he liked taking charge sometimes, the certainty of pleasing me fueling his own confidence. Our intimacy became a dance where the lead changed, a constant discovery rather than a fixed destination.

Two years later, I still don't find candles particularly alluring... but it's become our private joke, a reminder of the night we risked awkwardness, fumbled, and emerged closer. It turns out, the sexiest thing I can bring to the bedroom is knowing exactly what I want, and the trust that I deserve it.

Workbook

1. Beyond physical acts, how do you like to feel desired? What small gestures or words hold power for you? Reflect on what you receive, but also what you give.
2. Imagine you could change one thing about your intimate life. What would it be, and why do you think you've held back from asking for it?

Action Step: Open a conversation with your partner (if you have one). Not by listing demands, but through an "I'd love to know more about..." approach. Curiosity leads to deeper intimacy.

Chapter Eight

Motherhood Unveiled: Finding Your Way
An honest look at the challenges and joys of motherhood, offering support and understanding

"There's no way to be a perfect mother and a million ways to be a good one." – Jill Churchill

The baby monitor crackled into life, a high-pitched wail slicing through the fragile silence of 3 AM. For a blissful second, I debated pretending not to hear it. Then guilt, sharp as a papercut, stabbed through the exhaustion. I wasn't a monster, just a woman so desperate for sleep I'd fantasized about leaving my own child on a park bench with a note reading: "Please raise as your own."

I stumbled out of bed, a walking zombie fueled by adrenaline and leaking breasts. My four-month-old, Emily, was a blur of need: a hungry mouth, a soggy diaper, and eyes filled with bewildered misery. I rocked her, the monotony soothing us both—at least for the moment.

Back in my pre-baby life, I was the queen of spreadsheets and well-planned schedules. Motherhood, it seemed, was the realm of chaos. Where were the training manuals, and the Gantt charts? I felt like a fraud, clumsily navigating this new world without a map.

The mom groups on social media only amplified the feeling. A parade of picture-perfect babies with serene mothers. Glowing testimonials about the boundless joys of motherhood, accompanied by photos of homemade organic purees and impeccably tidy nurseries. It fueled the relentless voice in my head: "You should be happier...grateful...why can't you get this right?"

My friend Sarah saw through the facade. One particularly tearful morning, she arrived with coffee and a fierce hug. "Becky, you're a damn good mom," she insisted. "Messy, exhausted, and doing amazing even when you think you're not."

Permission to be imperfect. It seemed revolutionary.

Slowly, I started reaching out to other moms, the ones who offered commiseration over cocktails instead of cookie recipes. Turns out, behind the Instagram filters, we were all struggling. Alice with her colicky baby, confessed to hiding in the bathroom for ten minutes of blessed silence. Karen, battling postpartum anxiety, shared her intrusive, terrifying thoughts with a raw honesty that made me feel less alone.

We formed a motley crew, a lifeline forged through sleepless nights and playground confessions. We talked about stretch marks, leaking milk, and the strange, visceral fear that would probably never leave us. We shared babysitting duties, offering each other the gift of a few hours to breathe.

Motherhood, I realized, wasn't about achieving some mythical ideal. It was the relentless exhaustion, the moments of doubt, and the surge of love so fierce it knocked me off my feet. It was learning to let go of control and find grace in the messy, glorious imperfection.

There were days, of course when I just wanted to curl into a ball and hide. But then Emily would flash me a gummy grin, or doze peacefully on my chest, and that sliver of iron within me, the one I'd found in the aftermath of divorce, would reassert itself. I was strong enough for this, even on days when I didn't feel it.

One year in, things became less of a survival exercise and more like living. Emily babbled, crawled, and turned our home into a whirlwind of joyful destruction.

I discovered the unexpected pleasure of reading the same board book twenty times in a row and the simple satisfaction of a clean kitchen floor (ten minutes until a rogue banana inevitably splattered that triumph, but whatever).

I also learned that 'finding my way' wasn't a final destination. Motherhood was a relentless change. New challenges, new heartbreaks, and joys that snuck up on me. There was the first time Emily said "Mama", tears streaming down my face. Her first wobbly steps were both thrilling and terrifying.

Six years in, I'm still figuring it out as I go. But now, I do it with less fear, armed with a hard-won confidence. I'm part of a tribe now, women who see me, the real me, and celebrate both the struggles and triumphs. And on the hardest days, I remind myself that I'm not just surviving motherhood, I'm becoming a better, stronger, and more compassionate version of myself because of it.

Workbook

1. What's your biggest fear about motherhood? Write it down, then imagine your wisest, most loving friend responding. What would they say?

2. What is one 'mom fail' that still makes you cringe? Now, try to reframe it through the eyes of humor or compassion.

Action Step: Make a "Support Squad" List. Who are the people you can call on bad days, even just for a pep talk or distraction?

Motherhood is a journey, not a checklist. Support looks different for everyone.

Chapter Nine

You're Doing Great: The Truth About Being A Mom

A reassuring embrace for every mom feeling the pressure to be perfect

"The very fact that you worry about being a good mom means you are one." – Kate Winslet

The Instagram post made me want to hurl my phone across the room. Perfect children in matching linen outfits, building a Pinterest-worthy fort in a sun-drenched living room immaculate enough for a magazine spread. The caption read: "Soaking up these precious moments! #blessed #momlife #doingitall".

I glanced around at my own living room, a warzone of scattered blocks and half-eaten snacks. My four-year-old, Ben, was currently using his crayons as ninja weapons, complete with battle cries. I considered adding those to my own hashtag collection: #losingmymind #thisiswhywineexists #momfail.

Motherhood was a minefield of impossible expectations. Everywhere I turned, someone was doing it better, looking more put-together, their kids eating broccoli without a fight. Social media was the worst, but it seeped in everywhere. Perfectly curated birthday parties I couldn't afford, judgments about screen time, and those endless 'shoulds' from well-meaning relatives who seemed to forget what it's like to be sleep-deprived and covered in bodily fluids.

Before Ben, I prided myself on my competence. I was everyone's go-to person, the reliable one. Yet, motherhood stripped away any illusion of control. Tantrums erupted without warning. Days I planned down to the minute disintegrated into chaos. My carefully constructed image of myself was crumbling alongside the Lego towers Ben gleefully destroyed.

Emily's birthday party was my breaking point. It was supposed to be an epic superhero extravaganza, with handmade decorations and themed snacks. Instead, it became a frantic scramble. The cake slid sideways during transport, my attempts at a Batmobile fruit platter were laughable, and Ben chose that day to enter a full-on meltdown mode because his cape was "too itchy."

Surrounded by moms who made it look effortless, the shame spiral kicked in, fueled by Emily's disappointed face. It was Jess, always my voice of reason, who snapped me out of it. "Becky," she said, grabbing a garbage bag for the collapsed cake, "Kids won't remember the Pinterest details, only how much fun they had."

The truth is, I wanted to be that Pinterest mom. To have the energy, the resources, the sheer domestic goddess-ness. But comparison, as they say, is the thief of joy. And that night, I realized it was stealing my happiness as a parent.

That was my turning point, the start of my own rebellion against the myth of 'perfect motherhood'. I took photos of the mess, of Emily's frosting-covered face beaming despite the wobbly cake. I posted them online, a small act of defiance. The 'likes' were far fewer, but the comments from other moms were my goldmine: "Right there with you, sister!" and "This is real mom life!" and my personal favorite, "Vodka helps".

It didn't mean I magically stopped caring. But I shifted my focus. Instead of comparing outwards, I looked inwards. Did Ben feel loved, safe, and most days, entertained enough not to set something on fire? Yes, yes, and well, sometimes that was a 'win'. Our days became less about checking boxes and more about genuine connection. Mud pie baking instead of worksheets. Pillow forts over perfectly folded laundry. Belly laughs in place of forced educational activities.

I even started a blog, "The Perfectly Imperfect Mom". My antidote to the highlight reel. I wrote about the disasters, the tears (mine, not just Ben's), and those raw, clumsy, often hilarious moments that makeup motherhood. Turns out, I wasn't the only one craving honesty over filtered perfection. Other moms shared their stories, messaged me their gratitude, and formed a community in the imperfect trenches.

Motherhood is still hard. I doubt myself regularly, and envy still flickers when I see a picture-perfect picnic outing. But the difference is that now, I know it's a mirage. That real motherhood isn't lived on curated squares. It's in the sticky handprints on my heart, the sound of giggles better than any sound, and the quiet pride of knowing, at the end of most days... I am doing great.

Workbook

1. What's your 'Pinterest Mom' weakness? The thing you see others doing that makes you feel

inadequate? Now counter it: What's a strength that has nothing to do with external appearances?

2. Think of a mom you find intimidatingly perfect. Now, write her a note of compassion. What might she be silently struggling with beneath the facade?

Action Step: Make a list of 5 "Good Enough" Mom wins. Small things that went right, even in an imperfect day. Stick it somewhere visible as a reminder.

Chapter Ten

Your Path, Your Pace: Celebrating Progress
Let go of comparisons and embrace your unique journey and timing

"The only way to do great work is to love what you do. If you haven't found it yet, keep looking. Don't settle." –
Steve Jobs

There I was, a thirty-something-year-old woman at a Taylor Swift concert, surrounded by a sea of teens wildly flinging their arms to the beat. I felt both a giddy thrill and a nagging sense of 'shouldn't I be over this?'. Shouldn't I be at a wine bar, discussing grown-up things?

My best friend, Sarah, the one who dragged me along with promises of epic singalongs and ridiculous outfits, merely laughed. "Becky, who cares? Taylor is timeless. Plus, look around – there are women our age here too. We're not obligated to check our joy at the door just because of a number."

It was the 'Speak Now' tour, a perfect nostalgia hit for my high-school self. Back then, I belted out Taylor's lyrics with the certainty of someone who knew how her life was supposed to unfold: College, a dream job in publishing, maybe a charmingly messy New York apartment, and true love by twenty-five. It was a script straight out of my favorite rom-com.

Except, life stubbornly refused to follow the screenplay. My career path meandered, more puddle-hopping than a fast-track ascent. The cute apartment turned out to be a cockroach-infested fifth-floor walk-up. And as for love... well, my dating history resembled a graveyard of failed apps and lukewarm setups.

By my late twenties, the gap between my ideal timeline and reality felt like a chasm. Conversations with old friends became an exercise in dodging engagement announcements and baby photos. My victories - a hard-won freelance client, finding the world's best vintage dress on sale - seemed pathetically minor compared to their milestones.

The shame spiral was relentless. If I was smart and capable, shouldn't my life LOOK more successful by now? I scrolled enviously through photos of former classmates, their lives perfectly arranged. It never occurred to me that their smiles might mask their own messy heartaches, career disappointments, and those questions you only ask yourself at 2 AM when the world is silent.

"Comparison is a joy thief," Sarah declared after an especially brutal Instagram binge. She wasn't wrong. My inner critic latched onto these images as evidence of my failure. Yet, letting go felt impossible. It was a twisted habit, that ache of 'not enough'.

The shift began with small acts of defiance. Instead of agonizing over my single status, I treated myself to solo museum trips and fancy overpriced dinners with zero guilt. I explored hobbies abandoned years ago, figure drawing classes, trying (and failing spectacularly) to master a complicated pasta recipe. It was about reclaiming my time, and my energy, and reminding myself that joy didn't have to be tied to reaching some externally defined goal.

And there was Taylor, a constant soundtrack to my journey. Her music evolved, ditching the princess gowns and unrealistic expectations for a fiercer, more self-assured sound. The lyrics resonated differently now. Songs like 'The Man' became anthems about defying the boxes people tried to cram you into, while 'Shake It Off' was my go-to mantra for silencing self-doubt.

Then came the big shake-up. Stuck in a freelance rut, I took a leap on something unconventional: a job managing social media for...wait for it... a pet influencer. Yes, an Instagram-famous French Bulldog, to be precise. My 'serious career' friends cringed. I felt a twinge of embarrassment, then quickly pushed it aside. It was fun and challenging, and the pay was surprisingly good. Plus, who was I to judge what success looked like in the age of dog-with-more-followers-than-me?

That job led to others, building a niche I'd never envisioned but which suited my skills and quirky personality. Turns out, helping quirky animal brands thrive online was my thing. There were still days I'd worry that I was on the wrong track. But I was building something my own way, making my own timeline. And as Taylor sings, "the haters gonna hate... " best to drown them out with your own music.

So here I am, at that Taylor Swift concert, dancing next to my best friend, who's now married with kids, proving that happiness comes in many forms. Am I where I thought I'd be? Nope. Am I where I'm supposed to be? Absolutely. Progress isn't linear, success doesn't have a deadline, and sometimes the most rewarding path is the one you never saw coming.

Workbook

1. Picture your 'ideal timeline' – does it involve relationship status, career, etc.? Now, be honest: Who created that timeline for you? Society? Family? Outdated expectations?
2. What's a "small win" you discount but shouldn't? (Reading a great book, mastering a recipe, etc.) Celebrate that!

Action Step: Make an "Off-Script Wins" list. Things you're proud of that wouldn't fit the conventional 'life goals' checklist.

Chapter Eleven

Redefining Success: You And Your Family
Challenge societal expectations and find what success means for you and your loved ones

"Don't worry about being successful but rather work toward being significant, and success will naturally follow." – Oprah Winfrey

The invite sat in my inbox ignored for over a week until my elder sister Martha reached out asking how I was preparing for my family's yearly assessment (something I usually dread).

My family's annual "State of the Family" video call wasn't a cozy catch-up; it was more like a performance review, with my overachieving siblings as the star employees. As the day for the review came, I clicked open the invite, my stomach sinking. Attached was an agenda: Updates on career, relationship status, and vaguely ominous bullet point – 'Plans for the Future'.

Look, I love my family. But these calls... they were a special kind of torture. My brother the investment banker, effortlessly rattling off stock market wins. My elder sister, the lawyer turned stay-at-home-mom with triplets whose lives looked like a Gap ad. And then there was me: freelance writer, happily single, with a travel savings fund instead of a retirement plan. I was the family's lovable but slightly dysfunctional wild card.

I braced myself as we all clicked into the Zoom call. My parents' faces filled the screen, my dad looking stern, while my mom radiated forced cheerfulness. "Sweetie," she began, "So glad you could join! Let's start with updates."

My brother launched into deals closed, my sister showcased her kids' color-coded chore charts. My turn came, and I gave a brief rundown of projects, carefully avoiding mentioning the dog Instagram account that was currently my main client. Predictably, when the discussion turned to 'future plans', it got sticky.

"Becky, about this move to LA..." my dad started, the word *'move'* tinged with judgment rather than possibility. "Are you sure it's a wise decision, career-wise?"

I'd been dreading this. The truth was, the freelance hustle in New York was getting exhausting. I craved sunshine, a slower pace, and honestly, better hiking trails. My 'big city dreams' felt more like a default than a burning desire. But admitting that out loud, well, it might as well have been me announcing I was joining a traveling circus.

Before I could answer, my sister jumped in, "Darling, what about finding a serious relationship? It's not getting any easier the older you get."

I bit back a retort. Because 'not settling for another disastrous date' wasn't the answer they wanted. Instead, I smiled and echoed lines from Taylor's 'The Man': "I'm so sick of running as fast as I can, wondering if I'd get there quicker if I was a man."

Silence fell. It wasn't exactly applause.

The call ended awkwardly, my parents' disappointment hanging in the virtual air. Later that night, I lay in bed, staring at the ceiling. The familiar sting of 'not good enough' settled in. Rationally, I knew my life was good, and rewarding in ways they couldn't fully see. But emotionally, that little girl still craved their approval, proof that my choices were valid.

That was my turning point. I couldn't change my family overnight, but I could change how I reacted. I decided on a strategy of radical acceptance. They loved me, in their flawed, well-intentioned way, but their vision of success wasn't my gospel.

The next video call, I was prepared. When the inevitable questions came, I shifted tactics. Instead of defensiveness, I focused on the positives. I framed my LA move as an exciting adventure and talked about hikes I'd planned, and freelance connections I was making. When relationship probing surfaced, I'd share a funny dating app anecdote, deflecting with humor instead of taking the bait.

Slowly, it began to work. Maybe not full-on enthusiasm, but something shifted. They started asking questions out of curiosity rather than veiled disapproval. My dad even forwarded me a job posting from an outdoor gear company (my version of a corporate ladder climb, apparently).

The biggest breakthrough came during a surprise visit from my parents to my new LA apartment. Yes, it was smaller than they'd like, and the overflowing bookshelf was a cause of concern for my bookworm mom. But as we walked along the beach, my dad admitted, "You seem... happy." For once, there was no 'but...' followed by a well-intentioned list of ways I could improve.

Later, over dinner at a trendy taco spot my family would never choose back home, my mom smiled, a wistful look in her eyes. "You know, your Aunt Carol... she dropped out of college, traveled the world. We all thought she was crazy. But looking back, maybe she had it figured out before the rest of us."

It wasn't a full acceptance of my unconventional choices, but it was a crack in the wall. My success wouldn't look like theirs. But maybe, over time, they'd see it was a genuine success nonetheless. As for me, well, I'd keep chasing sunsets and deadlines, a few steps off the beaten path.

Workbook

1. Are your definitions of success your own, or inherited from others? What 'shoulds' can you let go of?
2. Imagine you're writing a letter to your 'younger self,' the one worried about being different. What reassurance would you give?

Action Step: Make a list of how you define success for YOURSELF. It's okay for this to change over time – celebrate that!

Chapter Twelve

Taking Space: You Deserve To Shine
Learn the importance of claiming your space and the power of being seen and heard

"Find your voice and let it sing."- Reba McEntire

It started with the little things. An annoyed sigh when I'd ask a question in a meeting. Ideas were praised enthusiastically when voiced by a male colleague, only to be met with a lukewarm "that's interesting" when they first came from me. I took a parttime job at a Marketing company while I handled my client's social media handles on the side. My office, the smallest of the bunch, mysteriously became the 'default' space to dump random equipment (but it was fine, I really didn't care).

It was the kind of stuff that was easy to brush off. Death by a thousand tiny papercuts is not the dramatic, headline-grabbing kind of sexism, but sneaky nonetheless. And I fell into the familiar pattern: work harder, smile brighter, be so undeniable they couldn't ignore me. It was an exhausting strategy with diminishing returns.

I'd always been the 'good girl'. In school, praised for being helpful and quiet. At home, the mediator, smoothing over tensions. My superpower was not rocking the boat, blending in just enough to get by. The thought of being seen as difficult, and demanding – made my stomach churn. Confrontation wasn't in my DNA.

Then came the big project, a massive rebranding for a top client. I'd spent months crafting the strategy, pulling all-nighters to perfect every detail. The presentation day, was me in the spotlight, fielding questions, feeling that rare surge of genuine confidence. My boss, Michael, hovered in the back, occasionally chiming in with generic observations, the kind designed to boost his presence rather than offer substance.

After, the clients raved. The project was ours, seemingly. That was until the celebratory email arrived – crediting Michael as the lead architect, with barely a mention of me. That night I didn't just cry, I raged. Not just at him, but at myself for letting it happen.

This wasn't just about a promotion; it was the realization that staying small had become a disservice, not just to me, but to anyone I hoped to lead and mentor one day. If I couldn't advocate for myself, what kind of example was that setting?

Sarah, as always, was my reluctant strategist. Over takeout and cheap wine, we dissected the situation. "Becky," she said, "sometimes niceness is just code for letting yourself be walked over." It was harsh, but it hit home.

My plan wasn't about becoming someone I wasn't – the office diva wasn't a role I aspired to. But it meant drawing firmer lines, refusing to let my work fade into the background. That required shifting something fundamental about how I operated in the world.

Next strategy meeting, I came prepared with a detailed printout, my name boldly emblazoned at the top. When Michael tried his usual tactic of reframing my ideas as his own, I smiled, then calmly said, "Actually, you'll find the original concept for that is outlined on page three of my document."

It was terrifying and glorious. His expression shifted, something between surprise and irritation. It didn't matter. I held my space.

It wasn't a magic fix. There were still moments of frustration, occasional sidelining attempts. But I was learning to play the game differently, finding inspiration in Taylor's anthems about shaking off the haters and refusing to shrink.

My next victory came not as a grand showdown, but as a simple email. A junior team member was struggling with a task, and I saw Michael about to hand it off to me. I pushed back, offering detailed guidance for her instead, with a gentle nudge towards figuring it out herself. He looked vaguely annoyed but consented. Later that week, she thanked me, cheerful: "I actually solved that problem myself! It felt awesome."

Turns out, taking space isn't just about owning your own accomplishments, but also making room for others to rise. I started offering more pointed feedback in meetings, highlighting contributions that were getting overlooked, and giving quieter members the floor deliberately.

It's ongoing, this battle with the old habits of self-diminishing. Some days I slip back into people-pleasing mode. But I'm getting better at noticing the signs, that sinking feeling when I don't speak my truth.

And now, I have the tools to fight back. Whether it's a well-articulated pushback in a meeting, or carving out time for my own projects instead of being perpetually "helpful", I'm learning that sometimes, taking space is the most powerful thing you can do.

Workbook

1. Think of a time you let someone else take credit for your work or ideas. How did it feel then? How does it feel now, looking back?
2. What's a 'small win' you have when it comes to taking space? (Speaking up in a meeting, saying no to a request you don't have the capacity for, etc.)

Action Step: Practice your "take space" line. What's the one sentence you'll use next time you're talked over or minimized?

Ladies, let's refuse to mute ourselves any longer. Let's take up space, share our gifts, and make some glorious noise. Go ahead, grab that mic, and start singing your own song – and don't you dare apologize for it!

Chapter Thirteen

Dreams Without Limits: Why Not You?
Encourage bold dreaming and the pursuit of personal aspirations, no matter how big

"Shoot for the moon. Even if you miss, you'll land among the stars." – Les Brown

Just before I turned 32 when I celebrated with a few friends; I had a major *Mindshift*.

It all started with a stupid pair of shoes. Bright, wildly unreasonable heels, the kind that make you question the sanity of their designer, but also secretly make a small part of you want to own them. I spotted them in a store window, a burst of glitter and disobedience in an otherwise sensible display.

The problem was that I was no longer a twenty-something-year-old girl who could justify such frivolous purchases. My carefully constructed 'responsible adult' life revolved around sensible footwear and well-calculated spending, not spontaneous fashion choices.

Yet, as ridiculous as it sounds, the shoes ignited something in me. Not just the desire for the shoes themselves, but a yearning for...more. More boldness, more audacious choices, more moments where logic took a backseat to something similar to joy.

I'd spent decades being the sensible one. Good grades, appreciably responsible jobs, the kind of partner anyone would be lucky to bring home for the holidays. My life looked good on paper, but lately, something felt off. Like I was following a well-marked path but had somehow misplaced the destination.

The shoes haunted me. So, in a fit of defiance (with a healthy dose of fear), I bought them. They sat in my closet, unworn, a beacon of unfulfilled potential. But they also became a strange sort of catalyst. If I could make one wildly impractical, slightly ridiculous choice, what else was possible?

The dreaming process was rusty at first. Hidden deep beneath the layers of practicality were the remnants of the girl who wrote bad poetry and devoured adventure novels. She'd been buried by the practicality of adult responsibility.

I started small, not with grand life overhauls, but by rediscovering those pockets of forgotten joy. A long-abandoned painting set found its way back onto my desk. I stopped hitting snooze, opting instead for those pre-sunrise walks everyone raved about, and, surprisingly, they weren't lying.

My friend Sarah, a lively whirlwind of chaotic energy, was my cheerleader. "Becky, you've been on autopilot," she'd declare over too-strong cocktails. "It's time to hit the manual override button." And she was right.

One drunken karaoke night, fueled by liquid courage and a particularly angsty Taylor Swift ballad, I confessed the big dream. The one that felt so impossibly foolish that I'd never voiced it out loud. Since childhood, I'd longed to travel the world, not as a tourist, but the slow, messy, soul-expanding kind of travel. Backpacking solo through Southeast Asia. Volunteering on an organic farm in New Zealand. Those Instagram accounts filled with sunsets over foreign beaches, I devoured them like a lifeline.

It was the kind of dream you relinquish somewhere between your first student loan payment and the realization that 'unlimited vacation' isn't quite what the brochures advertise.

But the dream wouldn't die. With every article I edited for those adventure travel blogs, with every conversation with digital nomads who'd crafted a life breaking free of the nine-to-five, the ember glowed brighter. Was this truly out of reach?

It took a year of what I called my "Year of Audacity". Every time I felt the urge toward sensible, safe options, I'd ask myself, "But what if...?" What if I took my freelance work on the road? What if I sublet my condo instead of renewing the lease? What if this wild, exhilarating, slightly terrifying life was actually within my grasp?

There were setbacks. The freelance client who bailed, the overwhelming logistics of downsizing my life to fit in a backpack. Tears were shed over sentimental possessions stuffed into storage bins, and arguments ensued with those convinced I was having a premature mid-life crisis. Yet, for the first time in ages, I felt a stubborn, defiant kind of alive.

The day I boarded that one-way flight to Bangkok wasn't about escapism or proving anything to anyone. It was about reclaiming the right to define my own adventure, to proving to myself that dreams don't always have to be sacrificed on the altar of practicality.

My travels weren't picture-perfect. I got lost, got sick, and got my heart broken a little (isn't that what those dramatic sunset photos are hiding anyway?). But I painted murals on hostel walls, lived with a family of coffee farmers in the Peruvian Andes, and learned to navigate the chaotic magic of Indian train stations. Along the way, I discovered that 'impossible dreams' are often just untamed ones. They require a kind of courage that has nothing to do with fearlessness and everything to do with proceeding anyway.

Many years later, I'm still a nomad at heart, with no immediate plans for a return address. My freelance work funds my adventures, and my client list is filled with fellow dreamers. Life is less stable, undeniably more chaotic, but infinitely richer. Sometimes, I miss reliable hot water and the comfort of knowing where I'll be a week from now. Then, I hike to a remote waterfall or share a meal with locals whose language I barely understand, and that old spark of wonder ignites.

The shoes, now slightly battered, remain in my backpack. A reminder that sometimes, a wildly impractical choice is the most sensible thing you can do for your soul.

Workbook

1. What's your equivalent of the 'glitter shoes'? That slightly ridiculous thing you secretly yearn for? Don't overthink it!

2. Think back to your childhood dreams. What sparked your imagination? What parts might still be worth pursuing, even in a modified form?

Action Step: Make a "Permission to Dream" List. Forget practicality, budgets, etc. Wild ideas only!

Look, dreaming big and bold is vulnerable. It's putting your heart out there. But you know what? There's power in that vulnerability. So, my friend, what's a "crazy" dream burning deep in your heart? Don't let practicality, fear, or anyone else rob you of that spark. Let's make "Shake it Off" (Taylor Swift approves!) our anthem as we step outside our comfort zones and into a life where our dreams have a fighting chance!

Chapter Fourteen

Finding Your Voice: The Courage To Write Your Story

Overcome self-doubt and find the courage to express your true self

"There's a real power in a woman who owns her own story." – Taylor Swift

The blank page stared back at me, mocking me. It had been this way for weeks. The idea was a burning ember in my chest, yet every time I sat down to write, the words would shrivel and disappear. My 'grand project' - crafting a blog about career reinvention, infused with my hard-won lessons. Yet, instead of inspiring others, I was the one paralyzed by fear.

Who was I to think I had anything valuable to say? Who would listen to Becky, twice-divorced (OH YES!!!), self-titled "expert at figuring it out as I go"? That nagging voice in my head, part cruel critic, part echo of past rejections, had gone into overdrive. 'Your writing is mediocre... your experiences are too messy... what makes you special?'

I've always loved writing. As a kid, my tattered journals hid messy poems and scribbled observations of a world that felt both too big and achingly small. Writing was my safe space, a way of processing everything I couldn't say out loud. But somewhere along the road, it became something I did in secret, never intending for anyone else's eyes.

My career followed a practical path. Finance was...fine. Stable. I was competent and liked by clients, but it never sparked the kind of soul-level excitement I craved. Through the turmoil of my divorce, writing became a lifeline again, late-night therapy sessions pouring my raw heart onto the screen. It wasn't elegant, but it was honest.

Then came the response that shifted something. A friend, reading a blog post about rebuilding after heartbreak, had tears in her eyes. *"This,"* she said, *"this is what you should be doing. Your words make people feel less alone."*

Logically, I knew she was right. The response to my online course about navigating career changes was overwhelmingly positive. I loved helping people reimagine their paths, and find the bravery to step into the unknown, the same bravery I so often lacked with my own story.

But there's a difference between being good at giving advice and putting your own messy vulnerability into the world. This kind of writing felt like peeling back layers I spent a lifetime constructing. What if the response wasn't empathy, but judgment? Or worse, indifference?

That's when I started digging deeper. What was this fear really about? Part of it was perfectionism, the belief that everything had to be polished and profound before it could see the light of day. But underneath that, there was the insidious fear of not being enough. That my rejections, my not-picture-perfect path, would become proof of my shortcomings.

Taylor Swift, as always, dropped some timely wisdom: "People haven't always been there for me, but music always has." I channeled that energy, turning my anxiety into defiant lyrics. Writing unleashed something in me – a playfulness that countered my inner critic.

Writing for no one but myself became my new ritual. Bad breakup poems, rants against societal pressure, love letters to my messy, resilient heart. It was exhilarating and terrifying all at once. Then, inspiration struck in an unlikely place – my spam folder.

There it was, buried under ads for suspicious miracle cures, an old email notification: "Your submission to the 'Voices of Resilience' writing contest." I had sent in a piece months ago, then promptly buried the memory. Yet, there it was, a little flicker of bravery I'd forgotten about. Why not? What was the worst that could happen?

Two eternally long weeks later, the email arrived. I won second place. My essay would be published on their platform, and a mix of excitement and terror washed over me. Then came the reader's comments, the real magic.

"I thought I was the only one who felt so lost in their thirties..."

"Your story gives me hope that it's never too late to change directions."

"Thank you for reminding me I'm not broken, just gloriously unfinished."

That's when the shift happened. Writing wasn't about ego anymore, or seeking approval. It was about connection, reminding people they weren't alone in their struggles, their yearning for more. My messiness became my strength. That's the thing about finding your voice: it's never just about you; it's about the possibility you ignite in others.

The blog is finally live. It's scrappy, evolving, perfectly imperfect. Some posts get a huge response, others barely a whisper. I still have days when the inner critic gets loud. But now, I answer back, using Taylor's bold confidence. I am not for everyone, but I'm for the ones who find solace, a spark, and the courage to write their unfinished chapters, because of my words.

Workbook

1. What's the story only YOU can tell? Don't worry about writing it beautifully, just get the heart of it down.

2. What's your hidden passion, the thing you do for pure joy but rarely share with the world? Why do you keep it hidden?

3. Think of a time your voice was silenced (childhood, a bad work situation, etc.). How did

that feel? How can you reclaim some of that power now?

4. What's your favorite way of writing? Structured journaling, free-flowing stream of consciousness, poetry, etc. Experiment!

Action Step:

- Make a "Small Shares" List – 5 ways to put a little piece of yourself out there. Sharing a poem with one friend, posting a photo you love, etc. Start small, but start!

- Make a "Fearless Writing" space. This could be a physical spot, or simply a notebook dedicated to unfiltered, messy writing. No perfectionism allowed.

Chapter Fifteen

Moving Forward: Healing And Growth

Find peace in letting go and strength in moving forward from life's challenges

"Sometimes the only way to get rid of the pain is to feel the pain. And trust me, you'll feel it." - Taylor Swift

The playlist was all wrong. Instead of the upbeat pop I usually blasted while getting ready, my apartment was filled with slow, sad, piano-heavy dirges my therapist would have applauded. But healing wasn't about being 'good.' Right now, it was about wallowing with a side of mascara-stained tissues and the remains of my emergency chocolate stash.

Six months ago, I'd have laughed at the scene. Sure, I'd had heartbreaks, but this was different – a deep, bone-deep ache. Because Sarah wasn't just my best friend since college. She WAS college, over a decade's worth of shared dorm rooms, bad decisions, and the kind of laughter that left your abs sore. We'd navigated adulthood together too, with all its messiness – career shifts, breakups, and those nights where a bottle of wine and endless rehashing of our problems felt like a life support system.

Then, the cancer diagnosis came, swift and brutal. There were hospital visits, chemo, false glimpses of hope, then the swift downward spiral. At thirty-nine, my lively, messy, fiercely loyal friend was gone. Just like that. Life had ripped her away, leaving a gaping hole in its wake.

The world kept moving, a cruel fact that initially enraged me. How could people be discussing weekend brunches and work drama when my entire universe had imploded? Grief turned me touchy, and raw. Well-wishers filled my ears with "time healing all wounds" and "she's in a better place" made me want to scream.

Part of me wanted to stay in this state, the cocoon of sadness a shield against a world that felt unbearably bright. I canceled plans, ignored social media, and retreated into old reruns we'd watch together, desperately seeking the illusion of her presence.

It was my mom, the least sentimental of people, who finally staged an intervention. "Honey," she said, her voice surprisingly gentle, "Sarah wouldn't want you to become a ghost."

Ouch. But she was right. Sarah would've kicked my butt, lovingly, and reminded me that joy was a rebellion too. Honoring her wasn't about living in the past, but carrying the best of her with me as I found my way back to the land of the living.

The shift didn't come overnight. There were still mornings when I woke up with the weight of her absence crushing. Some days the pain felt as sharp as ever. But I was learning that grief wasn't a fine line, it was a messy, swirling ocean with riptides and occasional calm days. Healing meant letting it move through me, not fighting the waves.

I went back to therapy, a practice I'd abandoned once I felt like a reasonably functional adult. It was still awkward, but there was comfort in spilling the ugliness – the guilt over the things left unsaid, the anger at the unfairness, the loneliness that clung to me even in a crowded room.

Slowly, I created new rituals. A Tuesday walk in the park where we used to vent about work, blasting the cheesy 90s pop playlist we ironically adored. I even attempted one of her disastrous baking experiments, finding therapeutic joy in the absolute mess I created.

There were small victories amidst the sadness. I signed up for a pottery class, a spark of the creative spirit Sarah had always championed. The first few attempts were wobbly bowls and sad little sculptures, but I was starting to enjoy the simple act of creation again.

One year after losing her, I decided on a bigger act of defiance. Sarah had always dreamt of a cross-country road trip, one we'd eternally put off for 'someday'. It felt terrifyingly symbolic to do it alone, but also the most fitting tribute. As I planned the route, old Taylor Swift songs became my soundtrack again, anthems of resilience like *ARCHER*... I was ready for this combat, it reminded me that I was stronger than I knew.

The trip wasn't some magical cure. There were tears shed in desolate gas station bathrooms. Loneliness struck at the most unexpected times. But there were also moments of awe - watching sunsets over the Grand Canyon, sharing beers with strangers who became fleeting friends, and the sheer joy of unexplored roads stretching before me. Slowly, alongside the grief, there was space for something else to take root: gratitude for having known her at all, and the stubborn belief that I could still build a life bursting with color, the kind she would have cheered the loudest for.

I love you, Sarah, keep looking after me till we meet to part no more.

Workbook

1. Is there a ritual or activity you associate with your loved one? Can you honor them with a new take on it?
2. What's a song, album, or artist that speaks to your grief? Allow yourself to truly feel with the music.

Action Step: Make a list of 5 things that spark joy, even small ones. Commit to doing one today.

Chapter Sixteen

Living Your Truth: The Freedom Of

Authenticity

Embrace the liberating power of being true to yourself in every aspect of life.

"The greatest act of courage is to be and to own all of who you are—without apology, without excuse, and without any demand that the world 'like it'." - Dr. Brené Brown

I got invited to my ten-year high school reunion, an event I'd been dreading for months. It wasn't just the usual anxieties about aging and whether my jeans still fit. Those I could handle. No, this was deeper. It was the fear of facing the person I pretended to be back then.

In high school, I was the definition of the chameleon. Desperate to belong, I morphed myself into whatever version I thought would get me a seat at the cool kids' table. I was the bubbly cheerleader, the angsty rocker chick, the preppy overachiever – a different Becky to suit whoever I was hanging out with that week.

The scariest part was, it worked. I was popular, always invited, and never lonely. Yet, under the ever-changing façade, I had no idea who I actually was. Likes, dislikes, opinions, dreams – all sacrificed to fit the mold. I'd become so good at imitation that it began to feel like the real thing.

Then came Sarah. Quiet, bookish, with a sarcastic wit that made me laugh until my stomach hurt. She also saw through my performance in a way that terrified and exhilarated me. "Why do you try so hard?" she asked once, with a bluntness that cut through my carefully constructed mask.

That question haunted me for years. College was a chance to start over with a blank slate, but old habits die hard. I still felt the pull towards mimicry, slipping into whatever personality seemed safest based on the crowd.

Then came the wake-up call, brutal and unexpected. A group project I'd poured my heart into received a mediocre grade. Worse than the failure was the reason: my contribution, according to the others, was "fine but a little generic." I'd once again faded into the background, so focused on pleasing that my unique voice became lost.

That night, I had the kind of full-blown ugly cry that rarely surfaces in adulthood. In the harsh glare of morning, amidst the crumpled tissues and smeared mascara, a stubborn spark of defiance arose. If they found me 'generic', well, maybe it was time to give them a Becky they wouldn't see coming.

Living your truth sounds like a nice self-help slogan, but it's messy in practice. It meant letting go of the need for constant approval, and the fear of not being liked. I reconnected with Sarah – a grounding force whose friendship felt separate from the endless popularity contest.

I started small. Saying "no" to plans I didn't genuinely want. Speaking my mind in class, even at the risk of sounding foolish. Embracing the fact that I genuinely liked nerdy documentaries and wasn't going to pretend otherwise just to impress a date.

Some people faded away, which felt painful at first. But those who stayed valued the real Becky, not the watered-down version. Discovering who you are also reveals who truly belongs in your life.

The upcoming reunion now felt like a battleground. Ten years ago, I'd have obsessed about the perfect outfit, practiced my fake-humble brags, and strategized to impress people I didn't even like that much. This time, there was a strange calm instead. Would I be judged? Probably. Did I care? Surprisingly little.

The night itself was a mix of surreal and...fine. Seeing those faces once etched so strongly in my memory, now felt vaguely familiar. There was the old urge to perform, but I caught myself and simply smiled instead. Conversations were refreshingly surface-level, free of the need to prove or posture.

Later, Sarah and I snuck off to our old spot by the lake. "They'd never accept the real you back then," she said, her voice soft. "Bet they're confused by who you've become."

That was when the real victory sunk in. Maybe I hadn't reached the pinnacle of 'success' as they defined it. But I'd gained something far more valuable: an unwavering sense of self that no one could take away. Looking back, I felt no pity for that chameleon girl, but gratitude. She'd led me, in her own clumsy way, to this place of authenticity.

As Taylor sings in 'Lover', "I take this magnetic force of a man to be my lover" – the real power comes when that 'force' is your true self, not a version designed for external validation.

Workbook

1. Think about someone who brings out the real you. What qualities do they have? How does your own energy shift around them?
2. What's a 'truth' you've been hiding? Might be something small – disliking a popular book, or loving an unfashionable hobby. Write about why you hide it, and the fear behind that.

Action Step: Make an "Authenticity Playlist" – songs that make you feel unapologetically yourself. Put it on when you need a bravery boost!

Chapter Seventeen

Body Love: Celebrating Every Part Of You

Shift the focus from weight to wellness and self-love

"My body is my home, my temple, my story. I will honor it, not fight it." - Virgie Tovar

The number on the scale glared back, a harsh reminder of truths I'd been desperately avoiding. Quarantine wasn't kind to my waistline or my spirit. Comfort food had replaced balanced meals, sweatpants were my new uniform, and the gym had faded into a distant memory. It wasn't just the extra pounds, but a dullness that had settled into my eyes when I looked in the mirror.

My body has always been a battleground. In high school, I was the skinny one, nicknamed 'twig' by less-than-kind classmates. Yet, I'd longed for curves, fantasizing about the kind of confidence they must bring.

Then college hit, and so did the 'freshman fifteen'. Suddenly, my body felt foreign, a betrayal. It became a relentless project: fad diets, hours on the elliptical, a desperate quest for control. There were times I'd see a goal weight on the scale, feel a fleeting satisfaction, and then immediately set a new, smaller target. It was never enough.

Fast forward a decade, and I was more frustrated than ever with my body. Work stress, a breakup, and then the endless stretch of pandemic isolation, had sent me back into old patterns. My self-esteem was directly linked to the number on the scale, and that number kept going in the wrong direction.

The rational part of me knew better. I preached to friends about self-worth, the poison of diet culture, all those empowering slogans plastered across body-positive Instagram accounts. Yet, deep down, the belief lingered: if I could just get thin enough, then I'd finally feel okay in my own skin.

Then, my niece, Lily, changed everything. She was six now, and a full-blown force of nature. One day, while playing dress-up, she declared, "I want to be a superhero with big muscles and a belly that jiggles!" She then posed in front of the mirror, striking warrior stances and making sound effects, radiating pure joy.

It hit me then, a lightning bolt of clarity: Children; before society teaches them differently, celebrate their bodies for what they can DO, not how they LOOK. When had I lost that simple, fearless delight in my own physicality?

Motivated by a cocktail of shame and a fierce desire for change, I did something radical: I stepped away from the scale. Instead, I focused on movement that felt good – long walks turned into jogs, then tentative attempts at videos of the perky fitness instructors who suddenly seemed less intimidating.

I overhauled my pantry, not with the mentality of restriction, but of nourishment. Rediscovering the joy of cooking turned into a form of self-care. Slowly, the obsession with weight loosened its grip. I started measuring progress not by numbers, but by how it felt to move through the world.

One day, a few months in, I caught a glimpse of myself in a shop window. I barely recognized what I saw. Not because of some dramatic weight loss, but because of the energy that radiated back. My posture was different, a newfound confidence in the way I held myself. That was the true victory.

Of course, there are still bad body image days. The inner critic doesn't disappear overnight. But I've learned to challenge her. When the old negativity resurfaces, I think of Lily, of choosing to be my own fierce, jiggly-bellied superhero.

Instead of agonizing over how my thighs look in shorts, I remind myself that these legs carried me through a half marathon fundraiser and that these arms hugged my friend when she cried. My body becomes an instrument, a collaborator, not an adversary.

I stumbled into a yoga class, initially terrified I'd be the least bendy one there. The teacher spoke of strength, of honoring your body's limits, and I felt something unfamiliar: peace in my skin. The final relaxation pose, which used to be torture, became a space to appreciate the simple fact that I was here, in this vessel that was far more capable than I gave it credit for.

Is my journey 'complete'? Absolutely not. Loving your body is a practice, not a finish line. But there's freedom in letting go of the pursuit of an idealized image. I'm finally starting to believe what Taylor sings, "You're the only one of you, baby, that's the fun of you." Turns out, it is pretty damn fun.

Workbook

1. Write a love letter to a body part you struggle with. Try to focus on its strength, what it's done for you, rather than how it looks.
2. Think of a movement you loved as a child. How can you bring a bit of that playfulness back, without the pressure of it being a 'workout'?

Action Step: Make a "Body Joy" List. Things that bring your body pleasure – dance, massage, a favorite outfit, etc. Refer to it when you need a reminder of all your body does for you.

Chapter Eighteen

Soothing The Soul: Beyond Coping Mechanisms
Explore healthy ways to find comfort and soothe your soul in times of stress

"Sometimes...the only way to let go is to lean in. To lose yourself in something bigger than yourself. To love louder than your fear." — Jennifer Pastiloff

The panic attack hit me suddenly. I was out shopping with Sarah while the kids were at their granny's. Then a wave of nausea and dizziness washed over me. My heart, a panicked drumbeat beneath my ribs, my vision narrowing to a terrifying tunnel. All I could manage was a strangled, "Sarah, I need..." before darkness threatened to engulf me.

Thankfully, Sarah knew the drill all too well (you see why Sarah's passing dealt me a very hard blow, she should be here today witnessing the strong woman I have grown into). With calm efficiency, she guided me outside and talked me through grounding techniques until my breath steadied. I wasn't new to anxiety – it had been my unwanted companion for years, rearing its head at the most inconvenient times.

Yet, lately, the attacks were escalating. The gnawing dread in the background had morphed into a constant hum, a soundtrack to even my most ordinary days. Work stress was the obvious culprit, the looming project deadline a weight on my shoulders. Yet, even when logically I knew the cause, the fear felt uncontainable, a wildfire raging inside me.

I was no stranger to self-help techniques. My nightstand was littered with books on mindfulness, and my phone overflowing with meditation apps. In theory, I had all the tools. But when panic struck, my logical brain short-circuited, leaving me grasping for temporary fixes and the illusion of control.

My usual coping mechanisms were losing their potency. Retail therapy sprees left me with a hollow sense of accomplishment and a lighter bank account. Binge-watching mindless shows offered fleeting distraction but fueled my insomnia. A glass of wine to unwind had turned into two, with diminishing returns and a creeping sense of unease.

The worst part was the shame. As a therapist myself, wasn't I supposed to be better at this? Clients sought my guidance, relying on my calm demeanor and carefully chosen strategies. Yet, when it came to my own struggles, I felt like a hypocrite, a fraud peddling advice I couldn't embody.

After a particularly brutal panic attack left me in tears, the realization hit me: I was stuck in a cycle of striving, not true healing. I'd turned coping into a performance, something to check off on my quest for perfect mental well-being.

Something had to change. So, I did the hardest thing I could – I surrendered. I canceled non-essential work commitments and gave myself radical permission to simply feel the discomfort without fighting it.

At first, it was excruciating. Sitting with the waves of fear without trying to fix them was a practice in excruciating patience. But gradually, I began to sense shifts beneath the surface. Instead of judging the thoughts that spiraled through my mind, I learned to observe them with a sense of curiosity. The physical sensations of anxiety, no matter how terrifying, were just that – sensations, not prophecies of doom.

I sought out a therapist of my own, a decision colored by both vulnerability and a desire for deeper understanding. She helped me unravel the tangled roots of my anxiety, the subtle perfectionism disguising itself as healthy ambition. We rewrote the narratives I'd clung to for so long, the belief that my worth depended on tirelessly pushing myself.

It wasn't a linear journey. There were setbacks, moments where old habits beckoned with comforting familiarity. Yet, every time I chose acceptance over frantic fixing, it reinforced a newfound trust within myself. True soothing, I realized, wasn't about achieving a perpetual state of zen, but about building the stamina to weather the inevitable storms.

I began incorporating practices that felt nourishing, not forced. Long walks in nature where my focus was on the sounds and sensations around me rather than ruminating on worries. Rediscovering the tactile joy of sketching, the perfection of the outcome is entirely irrelevant. Saying a hard 'no' to commitments that drained me, and the surprising liberation that followed.

One morning, brewing my coffee, I noticed a Taylor Swift lyric playing softly in the background: *"There'll be happiness after you, but there was happiness because of you, both of these things can be true*..." Unexpected tears welled up – not from sadness, but from a profound sense of self-compassion I wasn't accustomed to.

The panic attacks didn't magically disappear. But they lost their hold over me. I learned they didn't signify weakness but rather were my body's clumsy way of seeking attention, asking for needs I'd long neglected. In surrendering the fight, I found a different kind of strength – the strength of allowing myself to be held by the imperfect, messy process of being human.

Workbook

1. Are you fighting the discomfort? How does it feel to try surrendering to an emotion for a few minutes, just observing the way it moves through you?
2. What's ONE thing you can do today that feels soothing without striving for a specific outcome? (A walk, listening to music, simply sitting for a few minutes noticing your breath).

Action Step: Make a "Feel the Feels" toolkit. This could include a playlist of calming music, a soft blanket, a journal for unfiltered writing... The next time you're overwhelmed, use an item from your kit.

Chapter Nineteen

Many Paths, One Journey: Embracing Diversity.
Recognize and celebrate the many ways to live a fulfilling life

"We may have all come on different ships, but we're in the same boat now." – Martin Luther King Jr.

The wedding invitation arrived in a crisp, linen envelope. It felt heavy in my hands, more than just its physical weight, but the weight of unspoken expectations. Sarah was marrying her college sweetheart, a picture-perfect love story made for a rom-com. And while I was genuinely happy for her, a familiar ache settled into the pit of my stomach.

It wasn't outright jealousy, but rather a nagging dissonance. Here I was, in my mid-thirties, a decent career, a recently purchased condo... Yet, the milestones ticking off my friends' timelines seemed to highlight the blanks on my own. No white dress in sight, my longest relationship status was currently "complicated" with my demanding work schedule, and the maternal instinct everyone assured me would 'kick in' was stubbornly absent.

Every life stage felt like a multiple-choice question where I was selecting the 'none of the above' option. It left me with the persistent sense that I was doing adulthood wrong, missing out on some core component of a full and meaningful life.

On the wedding day, amidst the laughter and joyful tears, my unease crystallized. Relatives offered the usual well-intentioned, yet increasingly grating, "You're next, Becky!" The pitying smiles from those who assumed my singleness represented a failure rather than a choice. The forced joviality masked my growing sense of isolation.

Then came the speeches. Sarah's maid of honor, gushing over the couple's idyllic romance, held up their relationship as the ideal. It wasn't intentional malice, but the unspoken implication was clear: this fairy-tale love was the pinnacle, the path that ensured true happiness.

That night, as a Taylor Swift breakup song blared ironically during the reception, I slipped away for a much-needed breather. On the deserted patio, I found an unexpected ally: Emily, Sarah's older cousin, the forever aunt, known for her world travels and fiercely independent spirit.

"Tough crowd in there, huh?" Emily half-joked, offering me a glass of champagne with a conspiratorial wink.

"You have no idea," I half-laughed, half-sighed.

Emily's smile was both knowing and kind. "I've been where you are. It gets better," she promised.

The conversation that followed was the lifeline I didn't know I needed. Emily, in her sixties, had chosen a life less ordinary. There'd been long-term loves, but the desire for children or a conventional marriage never quite materialized. Instead, her focus shifted to building a successful photography business, the joy of solo exploration, and the richness of found family in communities across the globe.

"Happiness isn't a one-size-fits-all template," she said, a hint of defiance in her voice. "The world wants to convince us there's only one path, but that's a lie we need to reject. Our journeys are as unique as we are."

Her words ignited something in me. A flicker of anger, not towards my well-meaning loved ones, but rather at the narrowness of the expectations I'd absorbed. The truth was, I craved connection, but not in the ways prescribed to me. My life brimmed with love – for my rambunctious nieces, for friendships that felt like lifelines, and for work that, though demanding, had a sense of meaning.

It began with subtle shifts. Instead of deflecting questions about my love life, I'd steer the conversation. "Actually, let's talk about my latest trip to..." or "I'm actually passionate about this new project..." I took pride in my beautifully decorated yet partner-less home. I leaned into my role as the "cool aunt," indulging in adventures with my nieces that brought out my own forgotten inner child.

I even started volunteering at a local animal shelter, finding unexpected solace in caring for abandoned pups. The walks weren't glamorous, and the commitment was often inconvenient, but the tail wags and sloppy dog kisses filled a void I didn't fully realize was there. It was a different kind of nurturing than motherhood, but no less beautiful in its own messy way.

Inspired by Emily, I started a 'My Kind of Wonderful' scrapbook. It was filled with photos of messy dinner parties with friends, concert tickets, and postcards from my kids and nieces traveling the world. Each page became an act of defiance, a proud visual record of a life overflowing with meaning.

The transformation wasn't without moments of self-doubt. The loneliness was real at times, a reminder that choosing a less conventional path didn't guarantee immunity from pain. But I discovered a different kind of strength – the strength to define success by my own evolving standards, not by boxes society had designed for me.

One year later, at another wedding, I held a champagne flute high as the newlyweds were toasted. This time, the wishes for my own future happiness fell on more receptive ears. I'd learned to make my joy impossible to ignore. There may still be new loves, unexpected twists, or a redefining of what family means for me. But for today, I celebrate the vibrant, messy, ever-evolving fabric of my own journey. Because ultimately, the most beautiful destination isn't found on a map, but the one you bravely carve out for yourself.

Workbook

1. What's your "should" story? The expectations (yours or society's) that fuel your unease. Now, rewrite that 'should' from your own authentic truth.

2. Make a list of what brings you genuine joy, regardless of whether it fits the "perfect life" image. (Messy hobbies, silly traditions, quirky passions – embrace those!)

Action Step: Make YOUR happiness visual. A collage, a photo board, even just a list taped to your fridge – a reminder of what matters outside the standard narratives.

Chapter Twenty

Finding Your Hero Within: Self-Rescue

Discover the hero within you, capable of overcoming obstacles and achieving greatness

"A hero is an ordinary individual who finds the strength to persevere and endure in spite of overwhelming obstacles." - Christopher Reeve

The email sat in my inbox for a full hour before I mustered the courage to open it: "Congratulations! Your book proposal has been accepted." A surge of elation mixed with a potent dose of disbelief washed over me. Me, a self-published author? It felt surreal, audacious, a giant leap outside my carefully constructed comfort zone.

Yet, the idea had taken root with an undeniable tenacity. It wasn't a polished, neatly formed plan, but rather a persistent knowing, a beacon guiding me. After years as a therapist, my desire wasn't just for individual sessions, but to break down the barriers to seeking help. To take these often-stigmatized struggles with mental health, self-acceptance, and the complexities of modern womanhood out of the shadows.

The seed was planted years ago, back when I felt like I was drowning in my own life. It was in the therapist's office, in my own messy unraveling and cautious steps towards healing, that I first glimpsed the transformative power of being truly witnessed. It was a lifeline then, but also sparked something else: a hunger to be that witness for others.

The road to becoming a therapist was not without its own self-doubts. Juggling demanding graduate programs with my existing career was a logistical nightmare fueled by stubborn determination. The voice of my inner critic hissed those familiar warnings: "Who do you think you are? Do you really have what it takes?"

Imposter syndrome, with its special brand of insidiousness, became my constant companion. But somewhere along the way, another voice grew stronger. With every client who confided their own messy vulnerability, with each breakthrough forged together, the quiet certainty within me solidified. I wasn't just competent, I was capable of creating a safe space for others to do the hard, necessary work of healing.

The idea for the book, unconventional and messy like my own journey, aimed to be a guiding hand on the bookshelf. An honest exploration of the themes I'd wrestled with most – embracing imperfections, finding strength in vulnerability, building your own damn happily-ever-after. Not self-help clichés, but real talk infused with compassion and the occasional swear word – the kind of book I desperately craved at my lowest points.

The writing was a beast. Lonely nights fueled by coffee and stubbornness, staring at a blank screen until the words reluctantly flowed. Editing sessions filled with ruthless red pen marks over my most vulnerable admissions. But with each chapter, I felt a defiant thrill. I was putting something into the world that hadn't existed before, my own voice amidst the chorus of experts.

Rejection letters came too, some polite, some dismissive, fueling the familiar spiral of doubt. Yet, every time those doubts surfaced, I remembered the faces of my clients. The transformations I'd witnessed, the strength forged through struggle that had nothing to do with me and everything to do with the untapped power that resided within them. That same power, I realized, flickered within me too. So, I'd dust myself off, shake off the haters (external and internal), and keep going. Just like Taylor sings.

The book launch was a blur. Interviews, social media buzz, a whirlwind I hadn't anticipated. The accolades felt heady, the imposter syndrome temporarily silencing itself. But it was the messages that cut deepest: from readers saying it felt like a conversation with a trusted friend, that I'd made them feel less alone in their struggles. That was the victory. Proof that your biggest impact sometimes comes from the battles no one else knows you fought.

Ten years on, my office feels like a sanctuary. Each scuffed journal on the shelf holds stories of courage and resilience. The books lining the walls are not just theories, but reminders that knowledge becomes powerful when paired with empathy. It's here that I find my purpose, in the silences held, the tears gently witnessed. I am not their rescuer; that power always resides within them. But to be a lantern, briefly lighting the path, that feels like a life well-spent.

Some days, I still catch glimpses of that younger, insecure woman who walked into her first therapy session. Yet, that vulnerability transformed into strength. My own scars make me a better guide, proof that healing isn't linear, but always possible. I may never fully silence my inner critic, but she's lost most of her power. In her place is a quieter, fiercer voice that whispers, "You've got this." And most days, miraculously, I believe it.

Workbook Section

1. Picture a time when you were your own harshest critic. Now, write a letter from a compassionate, wiser version of yourself to the person you were then.

2. What's one small act of self-belief you can take TODAY, despite the fear? (Sending the risky email, speaking up about something you care about, etc.)

Action Step: Make an "Evidence of Badassery" list. Not just big achievements, but the small, daily acts of courage that often go unnoticed. Read it when self-doubt kicks in.

CONCLUSION: The Journey Continues

And so, dear reader, we've reached a gentle pause in this journey we've shared together. From embracing the 'now' to celebrating the extraordinary within yourself and others, we've explored the depths of self-love, courage, and connection.

Remember, the path to fulfillment is not a straight line, but rather a beautiful, ever-evolving spiral. There will be moments of radiant joy and times when you stumble. That's okay. That's growth. What matters is the commitment to keep shaking off the doubts, to keep nurturing that inner flame, and to keep moving forward.

You, beautiful soul, are enough. You are already worthy. Your desires matter; your dreams hold power. Embrace your unique pace, redefine success on your own terms, and celebrate the everyday victories along the way.

Never forget the profound strength within you – your ability to heal, to grow, and to write your own magnificent story. Let your authenticity shine, permit yourself to seek joy, and celebrate the very essence of being a woman and the experiences that surround you.

This isn't goodbye. It's a reminder that as you continue this journey, you are never alone. Carry the lessons from these pages within you like a guiding light. Wherever your next steps may lead, go with love, courage, and the unwavering belief that you are destined for a life overflowing with fulfillment.

www.ingramcontent.com/pod-product-compliance
Lightning Source LLC
Chambersburg PA
CBHW012054040426
42335CB00041B/2835